Closing Distances

Closing

Distances

Paul Martin

The Backwaters Press

Also by Paul Martin

Green Tomatoes, Heatherstone Press, 1990
Walking Away Waving, special issue of *Yarrow,* 1998
Morning on Canal Street, Foothills Publishing, 2005

Book design by The Backwaters Press
Cover design by Bristol Creative, www.bristolcreative.com
All poetry copyright Paul Martin, unless otherwise noted
Cover art "Purple Landscape," © 2009 by John Martin, used by permission

First Printing: April 2009

Published by: The Backwaters Press
Greg Kosmicki, Rich Wyatt, Editors
3502 N. 52nd Street
Omaha, Nebraska 68104-3506

thebackwaterspress@gmail.com
http://www.thebackwaterspress.com

ISBN: 978-1-935218-04-3

Acknowledgments

Thanks to the editors of the journals in which these poems first appeared.

5 AM: "The Neighbor," "The Burning," "Holy Water"
America: "Writing on Air"
Black Buzzard Review: "The Early Lessons"
Borderlands: Texas Poetry Review: "How it Happened," "Slovak"
Boulevard: "Mushrooms"
Boundaries of Twilight: Czechoslovakian Writing from the New World: "Closing Distances," "My Grandmother"
Carrying the Darkness: Poetry of the Vietnam War: "Watching the News"
Chiron Review: "The Blue Silk Sportcoat"
Commonweal: "The Announcer," "The Moment," "Horses"
Cornucopia: "Sweater Girl"
Country Journal: "Coldest Days of the Century"
Green Mountains Review: "Slopewatching," "Haircut"
Heatherstone Poets and New Voices: "The Butcher Enters the Communion of Saints"
Kansas Quarterly: "The Chickadee"
Louisville Review: "The Brown Patch"
Minnesota Review: "Friday Night Fights," "Talking to the Dog"
Mudfish: "Shooting Range"
Negative Capabilities: Words/Healing Anthology: "Delicate Boat"
New Letters: "A Cleared Space"
Nimrod: "Watching the News," "Her Cup"
One Trick Pony: "The Strap," "The Touch," "Saints," "Raising the Dead"
Poetry East: "Strawberries"
Poetry Now: "The Quarry"
Pulpsmith: "Young Lovers in the Park"
The Recorder: "Gallivanting," "A Different House"
South Coast Poetry Journal: "Closing Distances"
Southern Humanities Review: "Cutting Down the Plum Tree"

Two Rivers: "Turning the Corner," "Good Friday"
Yankee: "Burying the Dog"
Zone 3: "Brothers"

Thanks to Rita and Elizabeth for their faith in the poems and their years of encouragement and help.

Thanks to my friends who have read these poems and offered valuable suggestions: Harry Humes and Jim Murphy, both of whom have been generous and patient over many years; Len Roberts, encouraging from the beginning; Barbara Crooker, Jim Hopkins, and Steve Myers.

Thanks to my brother, John, for his cover painting "Purple Landscape."

Thanks to Margie for her encouragement; to my brothers, Mike and John, for their keeping alive the Slovak; to Lorraine Markosi Smith, whose reminiscing about the old Slovaks I miss.

Thanks to you too, Jacob.

Closing Distances

About the Poet

To Rita and Elizabeth

Slopewatching

Saturday night. Rain
on the tin roof outside my bedroom window,
and I'm back on Canal Street, upstairs tucked in bed,
the rain coming so fast it overflows
the gutters and splashes on the slate sidewalk.
Downstairs the telephone rings and my father puts on
his black leggings, his boots, his black raincoat
and cap, opens the door and enters the storm,
leaving a sudden emptiness behind him.
All night between the rising river and the dark brow
of the mountain, lantern in hand he'll walk the tracks,
watching for slides, ready to strike the bright flares.
Twenty-five years after his death, in a house of my own,
listening to night rain, I think of him
out there in the darkness and fall asleep,
expecting to wake and find him downstairs,
just back, dressed in his blue suit,
ready to lead us through the brilliant rain-washed light
to Mass, telling us to straighten our shoulders,
to lift our heads, to eat
those books so we wouldn't have to slave like him
and outside the church, after communion,
giving us each a small piece of bread
to break our long fast.

My Grandmother

I remember her flowered apron,
her hair pulled back in a bun.
No matter how early I woke, she was already up.
We were leaving the table before she sat.
She squeezed nickels into my palm
warning me not to tell.
Bruises blotted the back of her hands.
The only ice cream she liked
was vanilla.

Before I knew her, she had fifteen boarders.
She heated water in copper boilers
and scrubbed their heavy underwear,
her back bent over the steaming tubs.
She knitted, crocheted,
made sausage, *omatchka, kasha,*
flat bread sprinkled with salt,
waited up until dawn for her grown son
and if she stepped outside
she swept dust away from the house.

We have no pictures that show her young.

Haircut

(For My Grandfather)

He lifted me to the broad board
he'd set across the armrests,
draped me in a striped white apron,
tucked a tissue in at the neck.

The drone of electric clippers.
His faded blue workshirt
and short cigar
moving closely around me,

combing, clipping,
silver scissors whispering
in my ears, colored bottles
glowing in the mirror.

When he lowered me, perfectly
parted, clouded in talc,
back to the floor, the room was strange.
I stood confused, a new arrival.

The Strap

By the time I came along
with my blond hair turning dark
and my hopelessly open face,
my father had softened enough to joke
with my younger brother and me
and to kiss us each night as we passed
his desk on our way to bed, so except
for that once when I walked in my new shoes
through deep snow, I was luckier than my older brothers
and Geney next door who I heard gulping
for breath the black strap cracked out of him,
who learned to move invisibly through that house,
lifting weights in the basement,
trying to rush his skinny body.
In the meantime, if something he did
turned out wrong, to stand there and take it,

not do anything dumb, like that day he bolted
through the screen door two steps
ahead of his father, out the backyard, up the alley
until his father stopped, glared at him,
then disappeared into the house,
Geney out there alone, shuffling through cinders,
sitting, until light sank, on the railroad track,
looking up ahead, then turning back.

Gallivanting

Gallivantin' is the word we heard
those days my mother was overcome
by the urge to catch the bus to the city,

leaving behind that smoky town,
her cooking and cleaning,
to lose herself in the crowd

moving through the revolving doors
into Hess's, leading us down perfumed aisles
below golden chandeliers, stopping

to stare into a mirror
from behind brightly flowered dresses
she held in front of herself,

laughing with people we'd never seen,
then breezing out that store into the next,
her light voice trailing back

to my brother and me in shorts, scrambling
to keep her in sight,
growing harder by the minute to recognize.

The Touch

You can have your push button remote control.
Give me my brother's delicate touch
on the wooden knobs of the worn Philco
those nights he brought Hank Williams, Webb Pierce
and Kitti Wells from WCKY Cincinnati and WWVA Wheeling
into that small front room on Canal Street.
Those nights I lay on the floor watching
him turn the illuminated half-moon band
past the stationery needle to find The Shadow
who knew what evil lurked in the hearts of men,
Red Barber, the sounds of the crowd at Ebbets Field.
New York, Pittsburgh, St. Louis, Chicago:
his long, sure fingers searching them out,
finding the slightest crack in the static
that opened to clear voices beyond.

Who I Was

One late afternoon after high school
      basketball practice,
walking through the quiet halls,
I saw them, three old women in babushkas,
      dark stockings and sneakers,
emptying wastebaskets, mopping, polishing
the classrooms their grandchildren filled during the day.

The last ones from the old country,
all of them gone by now
and with them the Slovak I spoke
when I said, *Dobry den, ako sa mate?*
abruptly turning them from their work
toward me, wondering whose son I was,
their round faces slowly opening
like big, warm kitchens.

Dobry den, ako sa mate? — Good day, how are you?

Friday Night Fights

Sleepless, tired of the struggle,
I look out at the dark world and remember
my father, home from the railroad section gang.

His heavy shoes on the back porch, he sits
in his sleeveless undershirt at the supper table,
his body softening, starting to sag.

Friday night, but after supper he'll go
to his desk to work for the union, writing letters,
filing medical claims for broken, used-up men

before he comes into the dim front room
to watch the fights. There he stands, bobbing,
weaving, slipping punches,

the warm front room falling away
until I see him alone
in that gray light, digging left hooks

and short rights into the empty air,
groaning, covering up, always moving,
using all he knows to back

the shifty world into the ropes
where he can force it to fight,
finally, toe to toe.

The Early Lessons

Just when I think I'm finally free
of its gravity comes a dark face, dark hair,
full breasts and the limp pecker
flexes itself
and on it goes, this long war
that began Saturday afternoons with the nuns
telling fantastic stories: legions of angels,
dark rebellions driven down by Michael's sword,
martyrs singing in the lions' den,
Christ knocking at the door of each heart —
using all their patient explanations and threats
of endless fire to line us up, the whole damned
bunch of us, outside the confessional box.
There we stood, in the high tide
of our blood, counting up the same ones,
preparing to deliver their full weight
and promise again to stop
and behave like the saints who hovered
above us, weightless,
pale, impossible.

The Butcher Enters
the Communion of Saints

In babushkas and sweaters they come through the clouds
to greet him as he enters, wearing the brightest white apron
he's ever owned. Mrs. Johannes, Mrs. Matusik,
Mrs. Siska, the old women of Lehigh Street, all there,
and already he's joking with them in Slovak
and they scold him again for the times he pulled *Playboy*
from under the counter to show them
the perfect breasts and thighs and rumps.
How he made it they'll never know, but thank God
he's here, they tell each other under their breaths,
their ageless caucuses taking shape
as they wait, one eye
peeled toward him, trimming each plump roast to order,
throwing in a few marrow fat bones for soup,
food that'll finally stick to their ribs
in the rare, cool air of heaven.

The Announcer

On a balmy night my brother hunched
over an empty glass on the kitchen table
bringing us the Dodgers and Phils
from the Ebbets Field of his imagination,
my younger brother and me in pajamas
settling in with chocolate milk to watch
Don Newcombe stare in for the sign,
the outfield shaded to left or right,
infield back at double-play depth.
My brother's tongue on the roof of his mouth cracked
line drives over second and long fly balls
that curved just foul,
his voice rising and falling through quick
five-pitch innings and elaborate rallies
started by Ashburn's walk or Reese's bunt
that Jones let roll dead on the line.
Night air poured through the screen door,
my brother stared into the space
before him, the game building a rhythm
that had our father lingering over the sink to hear
Sisler digging wide around third with the tying run,
and here comes Furillo's throw, a bullet
from the base of the wall,
and there we are in our kitchen turning
toward my brother under the light

of the hanging lamp, the roar of thousands
growing out of his throat, his eyes wild and distant.

Young Lovers in the Park

This raw second day of spring,
they sit on the damp patchy green,
oblivious of everyone and everything
that moves around them.

He teases her, hiding
something behind his back.
In mock anger, she twists
her face into something so fierce
it causes them both to laugh.

Then she floats her kerchief
like a green flame
in the breeze above his head,
but he yanks it down
and binds her leg to his
with a knot at the ankle.

One arm around the other's waist,
the other boosting them from the ground,
they awkwardly rise
to try this new thing they've become.
Trying to run, they fall,
fall and again fall,
each time pulling the other up

til they work out this strange, stiff-legged
rocking rhythm
and heads tilted back, laughing at the sky,
they hobble into the distance
faster than you might expect
as though they could manage
a lifetime like that.

Turning the Corner

He'd buy an old car
and they'd lock up the house.

My mother would slide behind the wheel
and he, wearing his Cardinals cap,

would plot the way out.
That was the simple plan.

Forty years on the section gang behind him,
a cooler filled with ham sandwiches

and cucumbers packed in sour cream
and they'd be away clean,

down the block, turning the corner,
a bagful of hard candy, an unfolded map in his lap.

Saints

Lord, save us from sad-faced saints
Teresa of Avila

When Father Bermelin's voice came booming
up behind us, those of us in the back pew
of catechism class sank into silence
and one by one were forced to admit
that nothing was funny
about skinny Joey Narlesky's rubber face
and mimicking voices
and just to make sure we understood
where we were, he gave both of us one
full hour on our knees after class,
warning us not to move a muscle
as he tried to harden us into those saints
who stared down from pedestals,
not one of them cracking a smile,
not even the blue-robed Virgin cradling her child.
Even the resurrected Christ sitting on a flimsy
white cloud high above the altar
looked like he'd rather be back with his friends
joking and drinking wine by the sea
rather than here with his Father,
sitting on a separate white cloud to his left,
looking like Joey's old man after his curvy, red-haired wife

left him, sitting day and night in that same chair,
drinking, growing a long unkempt beard and hair,
eyes downcast and blank,
nothing that wild Joey did able to make him laugh.

Watching the News

From out there the news keeps coming
focusing here in front of the couch:
      mountains of shoes and eyeglasses;
      the limousine turning the corner — forward,
      backward, slowed down, enlarged, stopped;
      that naked girl running toward me,
      her back aflame with napalm;
these pictures that make it difficult to mow the lawn,
to replace a burned-out bulb or the brick

above the door where the starling returns each year
to build her nest. For weeks I watched her carry
each strand and now the eggs have hatched
on a narrow ledge inside the wall.
Though I can't see their blind eyes, their stretching necks,
I can hear them as soon as she enters the hole.

                              Last year
trying their wings toward the light, they tipped
the nest deeper into the wall.
At night I could hear their faint chirping
somewhere near the bottom.
I promised then I'd repair that hole,
but here it is another spring
and the starling continues to fly out and in

dropping food into the silence
and I can feel my chances piling up
like small, delicate bones in the darkness.

Mushrooms

This is one my father warned me not to pick
when he led me through these woods,

damp leaves spongy under our feet,
holding back branches until he knelt

closely over what I had missed, waiting,
his finger circling the white cap and the stalk,

describing the shape and color that made it different
from kinds that numbered into thousands,

pulling one he'd picked earlier out of his sack
to show me the kind we'd fry in butter

and dry for Christmas soup.
Look, he'd say, see the difference,

telling me how important it was
to open my eyes and remember,

looking over his shoulder,
calling me back from packed sandwiches,

the sounds of squirrels,
light flickering high in the windblown trees.

Poem
ending in
image

31

Sweater Girl

The most obedient girl
in parochial school,
she's turned thirty
and remote as those pictures
of saints the nuns awarded.

Finding herself among men
she blushes a halo
around her face,
lowers her eyes to speak.

On her white sweater a pale blue
bird extends its wings
to rise above
her breasts' soft slopes.

Up in the distant rim
of her shoulder three smaller birds
climb the thin air
heading, I guess,
toward a mountain nest
well above the snow line.

The Brown Patch

(For Kenny, Our Foster Son)

Looking through the rain-streaked window
at the budding trees, the grass turning green,
I see the brown patch you wore in the lawn
bouncing the rubber ball off the house
back to yourself.
From inside it sounded like the thump
of an insistent heart.
Was ours the third house? I can't remember.
But the day they took you back
we sat in enormous chairs at opposite
ends of the front room, a plain growing between us.
I held you close as I could,
then watched you carry your suitcase
out to the waiting car.
Now, two years later, I try to imagine
what we might have had, you and I,
but all I see is this brown patch
mottled with a fine, green moss.
Some days it looks like a blind, featherless
bird fallen from its nest.
Today it's a strange, unexplored continent,
a place I know only from maps.

"The Mystique of Attracting Purple Martins"

(from *The Martin Landlord's Handbook*)

For years I've observed the hundred rules
of the handbook and scanned the late April sky
for their sleek swerve
and circle,
their bright trill filling the yard.
One last try, I tell myself, as I clean
their white condominium and raise it back
to the choice spot overlooking the field.
If they don't show this year I'm done
with them and their many excuses,
like those guests invited to the feast.
Let the gritty sparrows have it, and the brazen
starling, let them descend
and settle in like the rabble
in the palace of a deposed king.

The Coldest Days of the Century

Ice glazes the inside of the window.
Snow, sleet, the ground gripped
so hard the dead go unburied.
All afternoon I sit at the window
seeing nothing, feeling this is the year
the sun won't make it north of the barn,
words will freeze in our throats,
our skins will thicken.

In the icebound house on long nights
we'll sit, each separate one, staring into the fire,
dimly recalling a time when our bare
sun-struck bodies floated on water,
when we picked dandelion flowers
using their yellow light to make wine,
dimly recalling summer before
it slips away like a dream
and we sink deeper into our bodies.

Shooting Range

It was deep into that row between
the tall tomatoes and sweet peppers,

down in that quiet place
of cool compost and tomato fragrance

my mind had settled
before gunfire from the shooting range

turned me back into the world
of loud headlines: those two locals dressed

in combat fatigues who looked straight
into the teller's face and left her behind,

one body sprawled across other bodies.
Later, I read they had practiced

nearby and I wondered if it was here.
Unsettling days in the country

of large, sturdy barns and retreating fields,
gunshots rolling in over the trees,

unhurried, deliberate,
hard to read.

Talking to the Dog

One of those high, perfectly cloudless blue skies
with enough breeze to sway the fringe of the maple
and I'm outside moving heavy stones, trimming hedges,
weeding the garden, talking, as I usually do, to the dog,
greeting him, asking him how he is this fine morning
and at the question, or the sound of his name
he lifts his head toward me, then turns away,
lays it down and sighs while I go on working and talking,
telling him it's going to be a hot one,
asking him what he's up to today,
marveling at the improbably green field
rolling out to the tree line,
asking him what he makes of this morning's latest slaughter,
whether the horrors will ever end
and we'll finally amount to something.
I wonder aloud about the orange dot
of a spider moving across my forearm,
the rich, watery song of the Cardinal
and the Flicker's bobbing like a dolphin across the field.
I tell him a story about the slow dying
of a large family and the terrible distance between brothers,
I stare into the face of his silence
and ask what it all means,
whether, beyond time and place, our smallest
gestures and voices are saved

and on I go, one day into the next, through the years,
working, praising, complaining, cursing,
talking to him, talking to myself,
talking to whoever it is people talk to
when no one or nothing is there.

The Quarry

Out where I live sportsmen stock the exhausted quarry
with trout. Two weeks later they circle the place
and like kids at a carnival, hook them out.

It's a loner who comes in the dead heat of July
stepping around shattered beer bottles to cast,
sit back on his haunches and wait.

Whenever I see him, his eyes drifting
out to an empty sky, I feel the slack
and think of the times I've seen him down

at the Ruchsville Hotel, silent at the end of the bar
until he gets drunk enough to tell me about
his ignorant boss, his ungrateful kids,
his twenty-year marriage going dry.

All he wants now is to fish, half a continent away,
a place so remote a bush pilot flies him
into a small clearing, a clear glacier lake

where he feels the line go taut across his fingers,
the sudden deep plunge into blood
until he comes back to himself, exhausted

and undivided, drinking and laughing with other men,
the thrill of wilderness just outside their circle of light.

The morning of her operation

I walked through the yard, past what's left
of the willow and remembered that summer day when

the saw ripped into the wind-damaged limb
and thousands of black carpenter ants

came boiling out, swarming up my arms
as I raced with the log to the pond.

How we kept cutting back, through tunnel-infested limbs,
light as sponge, the inside turning to dust

at our touch as we cut back and back toward the trunk
trying to find solid wood.

The Neighbor

In her old age my mother is passing on
the history of our block,
telling me about our neighbor who raised
six kids on her own by scrubbing floors
in Residence Park after her husband died,
the husband who beat her so hard
my mother could hear her pleading
through the walls.
"In those days," she says, " people didn't interfere.
I was just a girl. I'd hold
my hands over my ears.
Such a hard man he was. A hard man.
You never knew when it got quiet
what the quiet meant."

In the Fading Photograph

In the fading photograph you stand rigidly
next to your grown sons, a small
man with a tight smile who I sometimes think I knew
though I didn't see you drag yourself home
from the section gang to sit under the grape arbor
and take off those heavy shoes one more time.
But all these years I've carried you with me,
asking my mother, my older brothers,
stopping at your favorite bar,
and the closest I came to an answer
was that your second wife took what money
you saved after forty years of laying ties and driving spikes.
Some days the simplest acts make no sense:
the housewife rushing through another day
looks up at an empty sky
or a man in shimmering heat, the hammer
in mid-swing above his head, sees the spike
blur and the focus of daily life
suddenly drifts.
Proud old man, forgive me for thinking I understand.
It was a hot summer day.
Some dark stranger in you stepped up
onto the tracks and turned his back
or turned face full into the screaming engine.

A Different House

(for Mike and John)

What's the word for soup?
For church? For book?
And how do you say he's sick
but he's going to work?
The three of us sit at the table drinking beer,
testing each other,
paging through the Slovak dictionary
that opens the door to the house
on Lehigh Street where our grandmother lifts
the soup from the back of the coal stove
and pours it into nine plates with a *zhufana,*
where the men suck the *shpic* out of the beef bones
and *hlieb* is the bread our father kisses
when it falls from the table,
where smoked *shunka* hangs from the attic rafters
and the goose breathes in his tight pen
in the ground cellar.
What's the word for the quilt made of its feathers
we sleep so deeply under?
For the plum brandy our grandfather sips
those nights he tells us about the Cossacks, swords drawn,
storming across the borders?
What's the word for the way light gathers

softly on his broad forehead as he spreads the cards
in a tight circle, leaning two against each other on top,
and we take turns, starting at the edge, drawing
one card slowly toward us,
trying not to bring down the house?

Burying the Dog

Stepping out, I lean hard against the shovel,
my breath coming in frosted clouds,
then gather myself and continue with pick and shovel
down through thick maple roots
until I'm waist deep in the ground.

Then I carry him, heavier than I expected,
from the tulip patch where he died
and lower him into the clay, carefully arranging
the legs that ran like fire across these fields.

Before I shovel him out of sight, I talk to him,
I invent our own mythology, his and mine,
I tell him when it's my turn
to enter the darkness, unlike that fierce dog
who guards the gates of Hell,

he'll be the welcoming one
at the dim edge of the other side:
When I'm still stunned and smelling of earth
he'll come and lead me the way he did
when the two of us took our long walks
and he turned me out of the tangled woods
into the wide bright fields
toward home.

Brothers

He's my sick brother, but some days I swear
I'll close the door behind me forever,
drive away, never come back.
But I gather myself and go back inside,
and he, with reason enough not to,
apologizes and so we go on,
his limp right arm across my shoulders,
his left on the railing, we resume our slow stagger,
our crooked climb up the seventeen stairs together,
the brother who dreamed of changing the world
in a single, dramatic act
and the one who dreamed of needing no one.

The Blue Silk Sportcoat

image as metaphor
poem as metaphor
for world

On a morning I pull back my brother's sheet
to find him sinking into his bones,
and love grows more infected
with panic and blame, I drive away
to buy a summer shirt and slacks.
Three hours later I'm driving back
empty-handed, my anger building again
because the shirt I wanted I couldn't find,
the pants were pleated, baggy
beneath my skinny ass,
and the sportcoat that could've saved
the day was too expensive.
Christ, just once before I die   *turn*
or turn overnight into an old man,
I'd like to step out of all these troubles
into a summer evening wearing that blue silk sportcoat,
new summer shirt and slacks.
Freshly shaved, hair combed,
I'd sit at an outdoor café, drink wine,
watch people pass.
What would be wrong, just once, to feel
that first glow again, the false confidence
of new clothes, everything perfectly fitted
and matched, the crummy, fucked-up world   *rhetorical question*
unable to touch me?

49

Strawberries

It's ripe strawberries that bring me
to my knees in the garden this morning,

impossibly big and red as those
on the covers of gardening magazines in January

and almost as sweet as the small wild ones
my brother and I picked up on Best's Hill,

eating more than we dropped into the coffee cans
our mother fitted with wire handles.

If a cloud moved across that blue sky
casting a shadow, I didn't notice,

the snakes we were warned about
never appeared, and who could see,

even in that brilliant light,
beyond the quiet hills all the way to Vietnam

and the war he'd carry back with him.
Heads down we browsed through the field

until we were filled and drowsy,
sprawled next to each other in the warm grass,

juice smeared across our T-shirts,
our mouths and hands.

The Young Maple

From the kitchen window I stare
into the backyard where it flares

against a stand of leafless walnuts
under a gray November sky.

Each day it grows more radiant,
calling me like a pilgrim

out of my distracted life to wonder
at its golden light.

To think it's here in my backyard
where there are no crowds kneeling and weeping,

there are no faces or symbols in it.
Entirely itself, it shines.

Cutting Down the Plum Tree

The first full day outside while a neighbor spreads
a sapling's roots comfortably into soft earth
and another, just moved out from the city,
turns sod with his bright red tractor,
I sit at the green picnic table drinking wine,
sifting damp earth through my fingers,
rubbing it on my arms and face, preparing
to cut down the plum tree that throws
its dark, withered arms into the sky,
and already I know it will take all day
to do this right, to press my forehead
against its scaly skin and to circle it
slowly three times, first
for my grandmother whose plum dumplings sprinkled
with brown sugar filled my mouth with summer sweetness
and once for each of the children I lifted
into its thick white cloud of blossom
and who knows how many times for its strange
perfume that reached to the front porch
and left me staggering, weak with sweetness, through the yard.
Already I know I'll dismiss the easy logic
of pruning it down in parts and follow my heart,
cutting it once just above the ground,
and instead of letting it drop
and dragging it away by the trunk,

magic

I'll let it fall into my open arms,
the two of us standing there,
both trembling, its rough bark clinging
to my blue woolen sweater, me embraced by three thick limbs,
we'll turn each other in clumsy, slow circles,
falling into and out of each other, its brittle branches snapping
as we reel breathless and a little bloodied
across the lawn toward the fire pit
dark with last year's ashes.

The Delicate Boat

(A prayer for Fritz)

The stillness of morning.
Through the open windows
only the dove's soft weeping
as I wash my brother's face
and prepare to shave him.
He lies back in the pillow
and closes his eyes.
I look long at his broken body
and see, in his sunken chest and the deep pelvis,
in the high arch of his hips
and the raised curved ribs,
the delicate boat, so perfectly crafted,
waiting.
Along its sides the silent
waters are lapping.
Christ, all he could, he has done.
Let the waters rise,
let them rise and lift him,
drift him free of this troubled shore.

Green Tomatoes

The heart's out of me. What reason
is there to go in and eat?
Two months ago, planting this garden, I called
up to his open window to tell him it was warm
enough to plant tomatoes, his favorites.

Then there was hope
of getting him outside in his wheelchair
and rigging up some contraption to help him
drink a glass of beer and smoke his cigar.
I was going to bring him the first ripe tomatoes,
warm from the sun, sprinkled with salt.
I was going to lay thick slices
in between buttered bread
just to hear him praise the perfect gift of summer.

But tomorrow he'll leave for the home,
leave me standing chest deep
in hard green tomatoes,
looking up at a vacant window,
listening to the drone of a lawnmower,
feeling the seasons turn without him.

Horses

(To E on her Birthday)

On my desk a photograph shows the two
of us smiling broadly, my arm across your shoulders,
each of us holding a glass of wine
under the tall shade of the grove in Saratoga.
If I thought hard, I might remember
the year, where we stayed, at which
of the many restaurants we ate, and whether luck,
in the form of a long shot wearing our silks
broke through a wall of frontrunners
to run down the favorite by a breath.
The numberless details of light and shape
is a puzzle the two of us, on this frozen night
in quiet January, might piece together
into something like that summer day, one
of our allotted days that arrives like those horses
out of the distance, muffled thunder,
a torrent of muscle and color,

suddenly on us, and past.

Good Friday

In the end, the One
held up by water,
One who suddenly shone
and drifted free of the mountain
goes heavy.

In the end, his head
slumped to his chest,
flesh suspended from high bones,
he looks like my brother
reaching for each thin breath.

Now it's done.

The last cry gone up,
drained of blood
and hope,
he becomes the heaviest body.
Under his weight the strongest
shoulders shudder as rung by rung
they bear him back to the ground.

Nothing more to be done.
Look at him, sprawled
across his mother's hips,

then lower him in,
into the earth with my brother.

The Moment

Across the field
at a pond obscured by Black Willows

I turned a certain way
and saw a Great Blue Heron

beside a white limb
in the water.

Naked.
Uncertain.

Like the soul in its first moment
without the body,

lingering
over all it remembered

until I startled it
into heavy wings, beating

across the gray sky,
the place it left behind

emptied,
turned to something less.

My Good Clothes

My good shoes wait
in the closet. Above them hang
my one white shirt and a jacket.
The soul of patience,
they know that later
or sooner they'll be taken out
to a wake or a wedding,
maybe the odd dance —
they're indifferent to which.
All they want is light
and some moving air.
Until then they're content
to dream, though today when I opened
the door, the shirt looked heavy.
I thought I heard a complaint
under its shallow breath:
move, move, it seemed to whisper.
Soon enough we'll be wearing you.

We'll be stuck in the dark forever.

Writing on Air

The first time I entered his empty room
I stood in the silence

of the hospital bed, his white cup
still on the tray, remembering the day

I found him, my older brother,
in the front room on Canal Street

his back to me, writing
with his finger on the air,

unaware I was watching him move
from left to right down an invisible page,

pausing, striking out a line, revising,
until he turned and asked me what

was I staring at, was I catching flies
with my open mouth, then rushing

past me into his hidden life, leaving
me in that quiet room, dust

rising through slanted light, all those
words hanging heavily in the air.

How It Happened

A carpenter cuts two windows into
the attic roof, scattering the dark.
Another finishes the cathedral walls with pine.
But leave it to Rita, in between teaching,
cooking, cleaning, visiting the sick
and feeding her winter birds,
to paint the shadows out of the corners
and board by board raise the light
around herself as high as her arms can reach,
then climb the scaffold
and stroke by stroke, painting away the ceiling,
slowly ascend,
singing.

A Cleared Space

It's a cleared space that pulls me
off a back road in the Adirondacks
and draws me toward still visible base paths.
No one will mind if I step across
the foul line and walk to the mound.
And what if I stand motionless there
a while taking in silence,
then turn around to find
the fielders, each in position.
And what if I stand in the beaten ground
of the batter's box and without taking a swing
follow the deep arc of the ball
falling beyond the last glove.
I take my time rounding
the bases, staring into the dim faces
of a brother and friends.
I hear, high in the stand
of trees, the wind suddenly stirring.

Raising the Dead

She says she can live in the house alone.
When she's hungry she says she'll go to Mary's
and across the street to Johnny if her house needs work,
raising the dead to cook for her
and to keep her house intact.
I think of the coming years and wonder how many
long-forgotten will rise to their names
and be restored to their front porches, their kitchens,
their backyards tight with vegetable gardens:
Mrs. Matusik who baked for the rich houses of Europe;
Mrs. Luchman who invited her over in summer heat
for green bottles of Rolling Rock;
stout Mrs. Mihalik who argued politics with any man;
Theresa Stefko, her first friend;
the shoemaker, Mr. Malik;
and young Mihalitz, killed by a baseball.
One by one, rising through a confusion
of time into the streets and markets, shopping
for clothes and Sunday roasts: quiet Mr. Johannes, Shipkovskys,
Albert and Elizabeth Strbo, Tomans, Partels, Gazdas,
Petronella Selka, tall Mr. Mlkvy, Bohunickys, Havrans,
our cousins the Vidos, Slebics, and Siskas,
enough to restart the rusting plant
and to crowd the Sokol Hall on Saturday nights.
Already she hears the irresistible call

of her mother and father waiting at the front door,
wondering what's kept her so long.
One day she'll slip irretrievably past me
and walk with them through the smoky town to the Palm Theater
to watch the small man with the mustache and cane,
to play hooky and pick Jack-in-the-Pulpit up on the hill.
A tall, blond-haired guy she's had her eye on
waits outside the dance hall
for the brash, dark-eyed girl he's never met;
a family from Residence Park is advertising
for a babysitter and cleaning girl;
a son lies in an open coffin;
and down at the railroad station the newest ones from the old country,
all their belongings wrapped in horse blankets,
step from the train searching
for a black-haired girl who speaks their language
to guide them up the hill into their waiting lives.

The Chickadee

Despite all the aimless
pain, all the deliberate cruelty,

despite all the insane contradictions,
today I am happy, standing in the snow

under the feeder, barely breathing,
watching the chickadee, that old acrobat,

turn himself upside down to eat.
He comes so close I can see

the round seed on his tongue.
When I close my eyes, he flutters

the air around my head
and lifts me so completely out of myself

I can feel him fly into my skull,
a shred of straw in his bill.

Slovak

Maybe you'll hear it up in the county home
but not on Lehigh Street where strangers
occupy the old addresses and even

a simple *ako sa mate* puzzles
and turns away the few at the bar
in the Sokol Club. That world of babushkas

haggling with Johnny the butcher over
the price of a Sunday roast,
of backyards tight with vegetable gardens,

grape arbors and chickens' necks stretched
over the chopping block, the world of my grandmother
spitting on the back of my grandfather's hands

and massaging away the ache,
of packed 10:15 Mass and Sunday soup
and ignorant, stubborn grudges

that lasted up to the deathbed
and beyond has gone, word by word,
into silence. What Slovak I remember

there's no one to speak with, except
when I enter her still
undisturbed room to say *dobre rano*

and to ask whether she can breathe
freely now, to bring her news about myself
and the scattered family. There I sit

on the edge of her bed, speaking
the old language into the stillness,
she leaning as close as she can.

ako sa mate—how are you?
dobre rano—good morning

Her Cup

(for Elizabeth and Cathy)

At her blue and white cup in the corner
of the cupboard she greets me each morning
in Slovak and for a few minutes over tea and toast
I hear her, in between bites of her crunchy muffin,
asking whether I slept soundly
and where we're headed this bright morning.
It's the cup she bought at the lake, the place
she wanted to go even her last summer
when she had to be propped up with pillows
across the back seat for the hot five-hour drive,
then carried in her wheelchair down
the steep, slippery stone steps to the cabin,
reminding us how she once
chased down boys in schoolyard races,
kept house singing and swinging that mop
she called her honey across the floor
while listening to a stack of 45s,
sailed through dishes to thumb a ride
into the city to watch Gene Kelly dance away trouble.
With cane and walker and wheelchair she pushed past
the death of her son, her shattered hip
and the four strokes,
refusing to be left behind even

for the short morning ride for the paper.
Hold your horses, I hear her say, as she savors
the sugary coffee from the bottom
of the cup, the cup with the pink water lily
blooming between two steep blue waves.

Clearing

On finding my garden statue of St. Fiacre,
patron of gardeners and of those with various illnesses
(for Gail)

Raking aside last summer's straw mulch, I find
Fiacre face down in the warming ground
looking as though he's dead from the long exposure
to cold that settled in last October.
But now I see he's prostrating himself before
the climbing sun and the tall green flame
of the maple, so I let him be and go on raking,
ripping the brown spines of last summer's tomatoes
out of their tall cages, uprooting
eggplants and peppers until the ground stretches
bare around him, and he looks forlorn

as he did in that space
he cleared for himself in the forests of France
where he fled in quest of solitude
after the woman his father chased away
drowned in a river,
where he built a cell and tended a garden
and learned to lie so perfectly still
under his slate gray cloak trying to empty
himself into the Other he looked like a shell

when the first of the hungry and sick stumbled
into the clearing, and tapping him on the shoulder,
called him back to the world.

The Burning

(for Rita on her 63rd)

Just as I'm eyeing the wind-blown sparks
light in the dry pines, she piles on more branches
and declares it a perfect day for a fire,
using a stick to prod the flames higher
and already I can hear the volunteers screaming
down our curvy road the way they did years ago
to beat back flames leaping out of the hearth,
melting the plastic clock on the opposite wall.
You'd think by now she'd be damping down
but here she is, rolling on
years of dead wood that will burn through the night,
asking me to bring out the wine
she'll sip as she slowly dances
around the fire, dipping in
so close she'll scorch her hair and laugh
that laugh that has me laughing, helpless again,
searching the yard, the house,
something more for her to burn.

Holy Water

In a drawer stuffed with loose
Ace bandages, rosary beads

and stopped watches
I find the clear plastic bottle

of holy water I brought
from the shrine in Knock.

Full, except for the few drops
I used that day to dampen my hands

before I entered his room
to shave him, holding his face

between them, lightly,
for only a moment,

so as not to awaken
hope. The one thing left

to try before I let him go.
Why should I care now

not to empty it down the drain
and take it outside instead

to pour on the grass,
the unrelenting grass.

Closing Distances

The arbor, like a complex cross,
is up, the vines are ordered
and I'm ready to try to kill the pheasant
that steps nervously out of the field into our yard.
I'm ready to close distances
the way my grandmother did when she pinned
a chicken between her knees
and drew the blade across its throat:
the stiff, spasmodic beating of wings,
a rain of blood in the dust.
If I'd have been tall enough, I could've looked
across the fence into Siska's, Johannes's,
down to Matusik's and Luchman's yards,
seen chicken coops, pigeon lofts, smoke houses,
grape arbors, every vegetable garden and chopping block.

At the table on summer Sundays the sweat
of my grandfather's brow dripped into his soup.
He'd hold up the bone showing me how
to suck out the marrow.
After dinner he sat on the back steps, smoked his cigar,
his round face floating in blue smoke
above the pages of the *Zrkadlow* or the *Nevy Yorsky Denik*.
In the afternoon he'd take me down to the ground cellar

and lifting the thin hose to his mouth, inhale
the cold, sweet wine out of the barrel into his glass.

I'd like to think the town they're buried in
grows lush, abundant gardens,
that the mayor, a happy, shambling man,
makes his way from one to the next, pulling scallions,
drinking beer, talking with blue-shirted men
who lean on their shovels or adjust the nozzle's spray.

But all that grows is the number of stones
in the graveyard overlooking the town,
the gardens dead and rutted, poisoned by factory smoke,
and at 10:15 Mass where old Slovaks filled
the church with garlic thicker than incense
and sad, passionate voices that made pedestaled saints
tremble, their well-dressed sons and daughters
scatter themselves through the pews
and sing such a thin, bloodless song
the church feels big as a cavern.

I've lived too long in the distance of books
but I feel distances closing now —
the garden is overtaking the lawn.
Since I've broken the rake I'm on hands and knees,
breaking clods of earth in my fists,
the taste of earth on my tongue.
I watch for the sweep of his tail

out of the high grass into our yard.
I'll balance that small brain in my sight,
cry if I must,
throw him into a boiling bucket, pluck every feather,
save the longest one for my cap, invite

my family and friends for bowls of pheasant paprikash,
say more than an easy rhyme for our grace
and wash it down with the richest red wine I can buy
until I can get my own vines into the ground.

About the Poet

Paul Martin is the author of three chapbooks: *Green Tomatoes, Walking Away Waving,* and *Morning on Canal Street.* His poems have appeared in *America, Boulevard, Commonweal, 5 AM, New Letters, Poetry East, Prairie Schooner, River Styx, Southern Poetry Review, Texas Poetry Review* and other journals. He is the recipient of two poetry fellowships from the Pennsylvania Council on the Arts. *Closing Distances* was twice a finalist in the National Poetry Series. He lives with his wife, Rita, in Ironton, PA and teaches part time at Muhlenberg College.

LaVergne, TN USA
19 August 2009

PP4937400001B/1/P

9 781935 218043